ORCA
FOOTPRINTS

Listen Up!

EXPLORING THE WORLD OF NATURAL SOUND

STEPHEN AITKEN

ORCA BOOK PUBLISHERS

Text copyright © Stephen Aitken 2022

Published in Canada and the United States in 2022
by Orca Book Publishers.
orcabook.com

All rights reserved. No part of this publication may be reproduced or transmitted in any form or by any means, electronic or mechanical, including photocopying, recording or by any information storage and retrieval system now known or to be invented, without permission in writing from the publisher.

Library and Archives Canada Cataloguing in Publication

Title: Listen up! : exploring the world of natural sound / Stephen Aitken.
Names: Aitken, Stephen, 1953- author.
Series: Orca footprints.
Description: Series statement: Orca footprints | Includes bibliographical references and index.
Identifiers: Canadiana (print) 20210351829 | Canadiana (ebook) 20210352078 | ISBN 9781459827103 (hardcover) | ISBN 9781459827110 (PDF) | ISBN 9781459827127 (EPUB)
Subjects: LCSH: Nature sounds—Juvenile literature.
Classification: LCC QH510.5 .A45 2022 | DDC j591.59/4—dc23

Library of Congress Control Number: 2021948712

Summary: Part of the nonfiction Orca Footprints series for middle-grade readers, illustrated with color photographs throughout. Young readers will discover how to listen to the sounds of nature and what they can tell us about the health of the planet.

Orca Book Publishers is committed to reducing the consumption of nonrenewable resources in the production of our books. We make every effort to use materials that support a sustainable future.

Orca Book Publishers gratefully acknowledges the support for its publishing programs provided by the following agencies: the Government of Canada, the Canada Council for the Arts and the Province of British Columbia through the BC Arts Council and the Book Publishing Tax Credit.

The author and publisher have made every effort to ensure that the information in this book was correct at the time of publication. The author and publisher do not assume any liability for any loss, damage, or disruption caused by errors or omissions. Every effort has been made to trace copyright holders and to obtain their permission for the use of copyrighted material. The publisher apologizes for any errors or omissions and would be grateful if notified of any corrections that should be incorporated in future reprints or editions of this book.

Front cover images by Ben Queenborough/Getty Images
and Aliyev Alexei Sergeevich/Getty Images
Back cover images by Leonard Modderman, Compassionate Eye
Foundation/Getty Images and Walter Geiersperger/Getty Images
Design by Teresa Bubela
Production by Jacqui Thomas and Dahlia Yuen
Edited by Kirstie Hudson

Printed and bound in Canada.

25 24 23 22 • 1 2 3 4

A male red-winged blackbird perched in its wetland habitat. The defense call to protect its territory is an angry chak-chak-chak. ©LEONARD MODDERMAN

For Shyam, who taught me to love all the voices in nature's choir

Contents

Introduction 6

CHAPTER ONE
A BRIEF HISTORY OF SOUND

The Big Hum 8
Sound Science 9
The Evolution of Hearing 9
There's a Drum in My Ear 11
Ear Ye! Ear Ye! Ear Ye! 12
Talking Plants? 12
Underwater Waves 13
Language: The Power of Communication 14
Capturing the Waves 14

CHAPTER TWO
THE SOUNDS THAT SURROUND US

The Soundscape 16
Bioacoustics 17
Acoustic Signatures 18
Deep Listening 20
Neighborhood Watch 20
What's That Noise? 21
Natural Musicians 22
Noise Pollution in the Ocean 24

CHAPTER THREE
SOUND HEALTH

Healing Sounds 26
Noise!!! 27
Getting Heard above the Din 28
Noise and the Developing Mind 30
Ultra and Infra Sounds 31
The Power of Sound 32
Learning from Nature 33
The Search for Silence 34

CHAPTER FOUR
CONSERVING NATURAL SOUNDS

The Art of Listening 36
Recording in Nature 38
Acoustic Monitoring 39
The Sound of Change 41
Expert Advice 42
Conservation of Natural Soundscapes 43
Join the Conservation Conversation 44

Resources *45*
Glossary *46*
Index *48*
Acknowledgments *50*

Introduction

The author prepares a digital recording in the foothills of the western Himalayas, India. Ravines such as this one harbor a wide range of animal and plant species.
RETA MAE ZELIKOVITZ

We share our land and water with millions of animal and plant species. Individual life forms number into the trillions—into the quintillions if you count the insects. Each living organism, given the right conditions, emits sound. Every patch of land and each body of water resounds with a living chorus. The symphonies are rich and complex in structure, many having been orchestrated well before humans walked the earth. The melodic chorus of birdsong reaches a crescendo at dawn and rises for an encore at dusk. The insect rhythms are the very heartbeat of the seasonal landscape. Bees thrum, crickets **stridulate**, treehoppers tap and cicadas shrill. Even ants have their own songs. The world's largest mammals grunt and click their telegraphic messages over vast distances beneath the ocean waves, while dolphins whistle, shrimp snap and fish chirp. All of these sounds are maintained in delicately balanced ecosystems developed through natural selection.

Some mammals make their sounds vocally through their **respiratory systems**, while most **invertebrates** communicate mechanically by rubbing body parts together. Plants and trees make their own unique sounds, often "fizzing" as tiny air bubbles

Howler monkeys, usually loudest at dawn and dusk, can get very vocal when they are disturbed. This monkey is howling in a rainforest in Costa Rica. PETR BAMBOUSEK/SHUTTERSTOCK.COM

pop in their trunks and stems. Animal voices have purpose. They establish territory, attract mates, issue warnings and maintain relationships, their voices overlaid on the sounds of the earth, wind and water.

Sounds are like butterflies—they are quick to arrive and faster to depart. Yet they create deep impressions in our minds, charged with a power that can take us back in time. They also contain hidden harmonies that may lead to solving the biggest challenge facing humanity—how to protect the future of our natural world.

A dangerous new sound has invaded our wild places—the sound of human activity. Chaotic human sounds are entering **terrestrial** and marine **habitats**, disrupting and masking animal voices on land and in our oceans. This book is a wake-up call for readers to tune in to the grand scale of nature's music. I hope, for the sake of our living planet, it can serve as an ear-opener to those who read it and begin to listen.

A white-tailed deer in an Ontario forest, fleeing at the sound of an approaching photographer. If you had a microphone, you might hear the simple grunt that deer use to communicate with one another. ©LEONARD MODDERMAN

CHAPTER ONE

A Brief History of Sound

"Discover harmony where it is most deeply concealed."
—Heraclitus (c. 500 BCE)

THE BIG HUM

Scientists who study the origins of our world mostly agree that the universe started with an explosion—the Big Bang. That was 14 billion years ago. Most people have heard *about* it, but nobody has actually heard it. Until now!

In 2003 John Cramer, a physicist at the University of Washington, received an email from an 11-year-old student doing a school project on the **Big Bang theory.** He wanted to know what the Big Bang sounded like (who wouldn't?). The email got Dr. Cramer wondering too. He decided to analyze the **cosmic microwave background**, the leftover electromagnetic radiation from the Big Bang. Using this data, he calculated the **frequency** of the sound waves created during the formation of the universe. They were below the range of human hearing, so he made them billions and billions of times louder. What he discovered was surprising. The Big Bang wasn't a bang at all. When Cramer first played the sound through speakers, his two Shetland sheepdogs leaped up and started barking wildly at what sounded like an

An illustration depicting the evolution of the universe over 13.77 billion years, starting at the bottom with the Big Bang and moving up through time to the present day at the top.
MARK GARLICK/SCIENCE PHOTO LIBRARY/GETTY IMAGES

alien spaceship landing. After realizing there was no immediate danger, they (sheepishly) settled back down in the corner. The sound coming through the speakers was a deep, rumbling hum.

SOUND SCIENCE

Okay, let's get into a little sound science. All living things emit some form of energy. Sound is energy. It travels through dry air at over 767 miles per hour (1,234 kilometers per hour). So what happens if you go faster than the speed of sound? Well, fighter jets do it all the time. When a jet "breaks the sound barrier," it creates a **sonic boom**, a shock wave of 200 **decibels** (dBs) that sounds like a clap of thunder. To give you an idea of how loud that is, your whisper to a friend in class is about 20 dBs. Your ears will start hurting at about 130 dBs. But even 85 dBs can damage sensitive ear parts. So be careful with those earphones!

All sounds have a frequency, determined by how many sound waves are created per second. When the time between waves is short—in other words, the waves come more often—the sound is high in frequency. When the waves are slow, or less frequent, they produce a low note or frequency. Humans hear sounds between 20 hertz (Hz)—a hertz is one cycle or beat per second—and 20,000 hertz (20 kHz). Some animals, like tarsiers and dolphins, communicate at higher frequencies, so we don't hear all of their calls. Others, like giraffes and alligators, can communicate at frequencies lower than the human hearing range.

THE EVOLUTION OF HEARING

So what were the first animals to evolve the ability to hear? Biologists who study evolution believe that bony fishes were the first to hear, around 400 million years ago. The fish adapted a mechanism they used to keep themselves upright in water into a means of detecting sound waves—in other words, hearing.

SOUND BITE

Have you ever wondered what it sounds like on the moon? Outer space is a *vacuum*, with only a few scattered atoms floating around. Atoms need to touch each other for sound to be transmitted. That's why on the moon you won't hear a thing.

A fighter jet breaks the sound barrier. Shock waves cause condensation of water vapor in the air, resulting in a halo-like effect around the plane.
KATERINA_S/SHUTTERSTOCK.COM

SOUND BITE

Spiders have eight legs—all the better to hear you with. Fishing spiders use their hairy legs to "hear" approaching bullfrogs and avoid being gobbled up in the flick of a tongue.

As animals moved onto land, they developed new body parts for hearing in air. Inner ears and eardrums started to appear. Slowly, specialized hearing organs appeared in animals, from spiders to rodents and elephants, living in a wide variety of habitats. Some animals took to the air. Bats, the only mammals to fly, developed *echolocation*. Elephants, on the other hand, not inclined to aerobatics, learned to communicate at the low end of the frequency scale. Sensitive nerve endings in their huge feet pick up sound vibrations traveling through the ground. Hundreds of thousands of other hearing and vocalization mechanisms evolved throughout the animal kingdom—and the plants were listening too!

A female emerald jumping spider, about 0.3 to 0.5 inches (8 to 12 millimeters) in length. Very fine white hairs called trichobothria, found on the legs of some spiders (inset), help them "hear."
TOP: STEPHEN JOHNSON; INSET: JIM MCLEAN

Bats use echolocation to navigate and locate their insect prey. These high-frequency sounds are above humans' hearing range.
JOHNER IMAGES/GETTY IMAGES

Sound Research

Dr. Caitlin O'Connell has studied the low-frequency calls of Namibia's elephants for many years. Her research team broadcasts a recorded version of the elephants' alarm calls using a device called a shaker that is buried in the ground. A geophone, an instrument used to detect ground vibrations, records how much sound reaches the elephants. When they hear the recorded alarm call, the elephants go into alert mode and then flee the area. The scientists found that the elephants can detect low-frequency sounds transmitted through the earth from miles away. The huge pads on the bottom of the elephant's feet pick up vibrations from the ground and send the signals all the way up to the animal's brain. These sounds are inaudible to humans.

ELI SOLIDUM/WIKIMEDIA COMMONS/CC BY-SA 4.0

THERE'S A DRUM IN MY EAR

Many animals, including humans, have ears on each side of their head to help determine the location of sounds. So how do our ears work? When sound enters the ear, it travels along a small canal to the eardrum, a thin, tightly stretched membrane that vibrates when sound waves hit it. The drum triggers a series of bones, the malleus, incus and staples, in the middle ear. In a healthy ear they *amplify* the sound, making it up to a thousand times louder. The *cochlea*, a spiral mechanism in the inner ear, converts the waves from air to fluid. Tiny hairs immersed in a saltwater-like fluid (remember our marine ancestors?) then transform the sound into an electrical signal that travels along the nerves to the brain. A leopard's growl, a bee's buzz or your mother's voice—each sound sparks a different reaction that can either stop you in your tracks or spur your body into action.

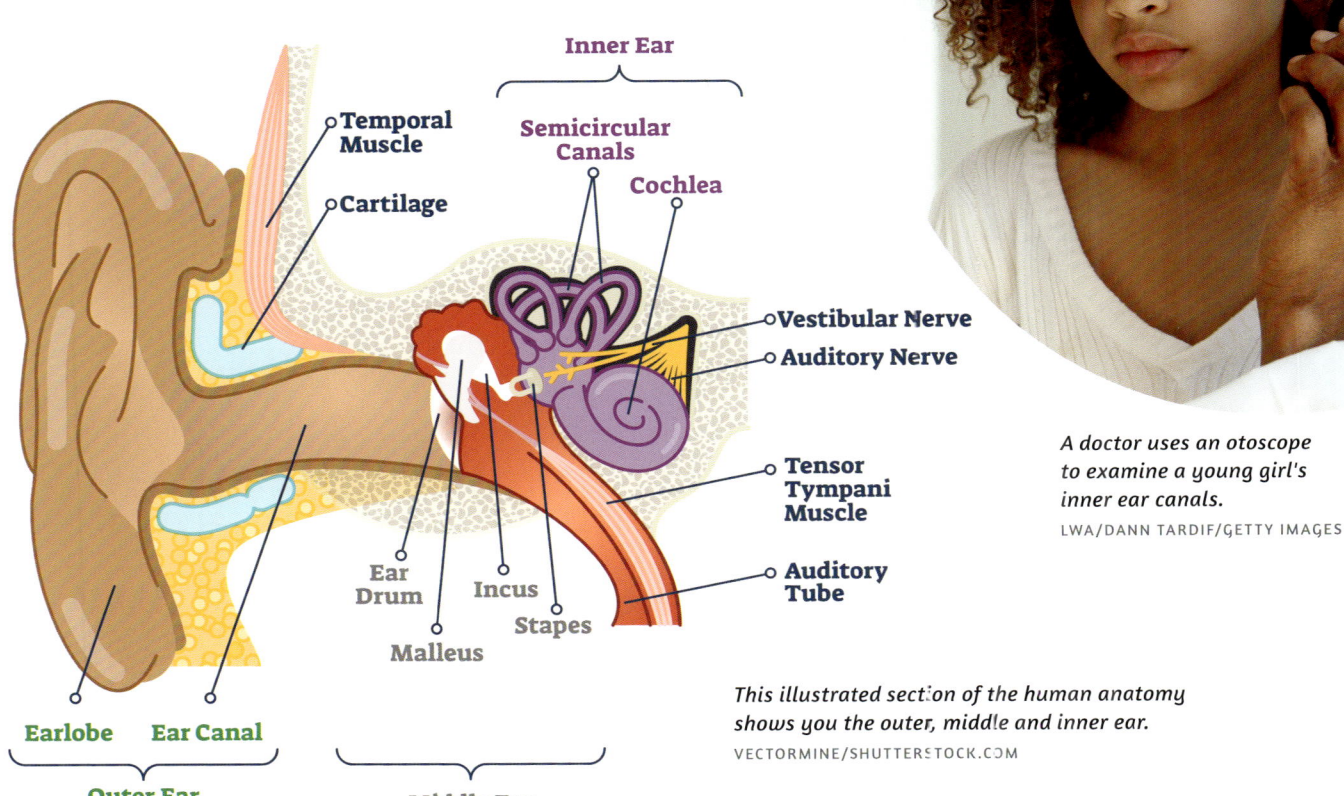

A doctor uses an otoscope to examine a young girl's inner ear canals.
LWA/DANN TARDIF/GETTY IMAGES

This illustrated section of the human anatomy shows you the outer, middle and inner ear.
VECTORMINE/SHUTTERSTOCK.COM

Large ears give the snowshoe hare excellent hearing. In the warm weather, the ears fill with blood to help keep the animal cool.
© LEONARD MODDERMAN

SOUND BITE

Snakes don't have outer ears. They pick up vibrations in their jawbones and send them on to the inner ear. Many animals hear with the help of their skull bones, including humans, especially when swimming underwater.

EAR YE! EAR YE! EAR YE!

Animal ears come in a wide variety of shapes and sizes. The ear's structure is determined by where an animal lives and who its friends and enemies are. Take rabbits and hares, for example. A hare's towering ears are perched like antennae on the top of its head, enabling it to hear sounds from as far away as 2 miles (3.2 kilometers)—a good thing because its only defense is a quick exit! Each rabbit ear can rotate to pick up sounds from almost every direction.

Studies of dogs show that their hearing is so sensitive they can pick up the high-pitched vibrations of termites inside house walls. I'm not sure I would want that kind of hearing, but you have to admit it's impressive. Cats also have super hearing, picking up even higher-pitched sounds than dogs do. That's probably what keeps them one step ahead. But if it's an owl the cats are hunting, they might have a hard time going undetected. Many owls have cockeyed ears—one ear is located slightly forward from the other. During flight, the owl uses its left ear to pick up sounds from the ground while the right ear tilts upward to hear sounds from above. Now that's custom design!

TALKING PLANTS?

I always knew the plants in my garden were good listeners, but I never imagined that plants could talk back. Specialized recorders have shown that tobacco and tomato plants make airborne sounds, particularly when they're under stress. They don't have vocal cords (obviously), and the sounds can't be heard by the human ear, but water-starved tomato plants make up to 35 cries an hour. That's a lot of crying! Unstressed plants, on the other hand, average fewer than one sound per hour. All the plant's cries are in the *ultrasonic* range, but just because humans don't hear these sounds doesn't mean that insects and other animals don't. As climate change heats up our planet, listening to the needs of food plants might become increasingly important to feed an overpopulated world.

The work of Australian scientist Monica Gagliano suggests that plants actively "hear." Using a recording of the sound of water, one of her groundbreaking experiments showed that plant roots will grow toward the water sound, suggesting that sound waves play an important role in how plants grow.

UNDERWATER WAVES

Have you ever noticed how strange your hearing is underwater? That's because aquatic sounds don't travel through the inner ear. They vibrate against the skull bone just behind your outer ear. So how do marine animals hear? Sharks have three semicircular canals lined with tiny hairs inside their heads. The sensitive hairs help pick up low-frequency vibrations in the water.

Sperm whales are among the loudest animals on the planet. They produce buzzes, clicks and squeaks from their bulbous, oil-filled heads. A complex set of organs, air passages, fatty tissue and a pair of clappers called "monkey lips" near the front of the head (seriously!) all play a role in how the whale makes sounds. When sperm whales gather with other members of their clan, they make special patterns of clicks called codas. Scientists can recognize a vocal clan through these codas even though the whales may be thousands of kilometers apart.

Two tiger sharks feed silently on the ocean floor. No one has ever found a sound-making organ in a shark. They do, however, let out a fart of air when they want to dive deeper in the water.
LE BOUIL BAPTISTE/SHUTTERSTOCK.COM

A mother sperm whale uses a completely different set of clicks to communicate with her calf (right). Inset graphic: Cross section of a sperm whale's head, revealing the internal organs, sacs and air passages.
GRAPHIC: KURZON/WIKIMEDIA COMMONS/ CC BY-SA 2.0
SPERM WHALES: GABR EL BARATHIEU/ WIKIMEDIA COMMONS/CC BY-SA 2.0

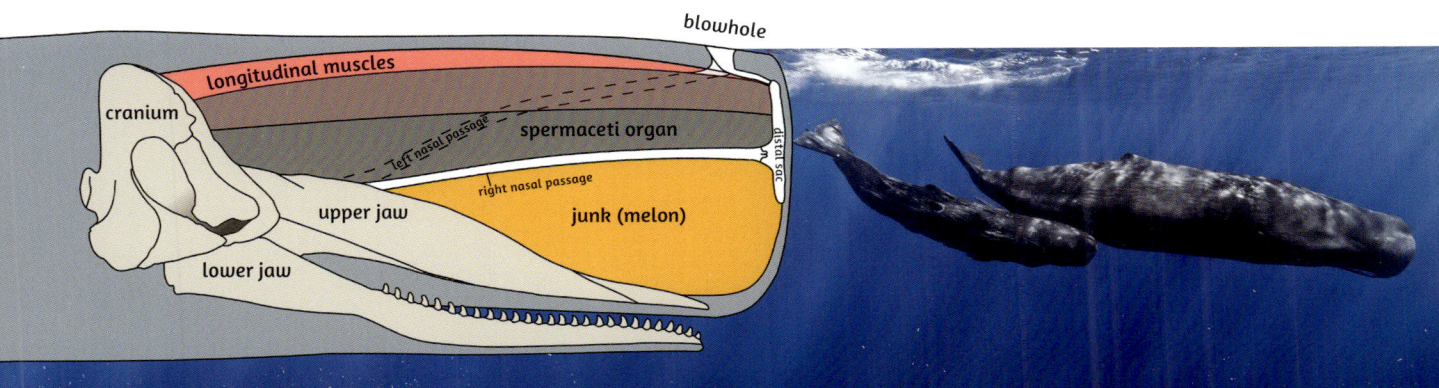

Two young girls share some stories after class. We learn the power of words at a very young age.
WESTEND61/GETTY IMAGES

LANGUAGE: THE POWER OF COMMUNICATION

Animals make many different kinds of sounds to communicate with each other. They roar, squeak, howl, hoot, hiss, gobble, buzz, bleat, trumpet, bray, oink, squeal, growl, purr, honk, bark, chirp, click and quack. Recently captured video reveals what appears to be an entirely new species of beaked whales. The sound of their calls is being used to help confirm the discovery.

Famous primate biologist Jane Goodall has demonstrated the broad emotional range of chimpanzee communication. We humans share a surprising number of vocal and behavioral characteristics with great apes. Human language has evolved further to become the most successful means of communication in the entire evolutionary history of our planet. The spoken and written word has enabled humans to work together, build communities, unite people around the world with a common cause, exchange ideas and share hopes and dreams.

Speaking requires fine motor control over the vocal cords and vocal tract. Special nerves link the voice box to the motor cortex of the brain. Some theorists of language evolution believe that early humans learned to sing before speaking. They point to the child's brain and how children learn words through rhyming fairy tales.

CAPTURING THE WAVES

A huge leap in human communication took place in the 19th century with the invention of devices that recorded sound. It was 1857 when inventor Édouard-Léon Scott de Martinville made the earliest known sound-recording device, a **phonautograph**. Thomas Edison later invented a device that could both record and replay spoken words and music.

Alexander Graham Bell invented the telephone and in 1876 made the first phone call to his assistant, Thomas Watson.

Alexander Graham Bell makes a telephone call at the opening of the long-distance line from New York to Chicago in 1892.
FOX PHOTOS/GETTY IMAGES

Bell reportedly said, "Mr. Watson, come here. I want to see you." Though Bell's statement may have appeared unimaginative to some, that phone call changed the world. Thirty years later on Christmas Eve, from a 400-foot transmitting tower built at Brant Rock, Massachusetts, Canadian scientist Reginald Fessenden, the "Father of Voice Radio," made the first public wireless broadcast. It went all the way out to ships in the Atlantic Ocean. The Christmas concert was the highlight of Fessenden's lifelong ambition to transmit sound without wires. To those on the ships at the time, it created a truly magical Christmas celebration.

Wireless sound technology rose to a new level when Martin Cooper, working for Motorola in 1973, stood on a street corner in New York City and made the first mobile phone call. In less than 30 years, cell phones overtook landlines in worldwide usage. Today, in any city in the world, you would have a difficult time finding a street corner without someone talking on a cell phone.

Our growing cities are becoming overwhelmed with the sounds of human activity. It is starting to spill into the countryside, drowning out the rich tapestry of sounds made by wild animals of all shapes and sizes.

Many people spend a lot of time texting and talking on their phones. Some psychologists fear that social skills for communicating directly with people are in decline. What do you think?
JESSIE CASSON/GETTY IMAGES

A girl talks on a cell phone while walking on a crowded city street. Talking and texting while doing other activities can be distracting and has led to many accidents and injuries. Hearing and seeing our surrounding environment requires attention. GEORGECLERK/GETTY IMAGES

CHAPTER TWO

The Sounds That Surround Us

"Now I will do nothing but listen . . . I hear all sounds running together, combined, fused or following, sounds of the city and sounds out of the city, sounds of the day and night . . ."
—Walt Whitman, "Song of Myself, 26"

THE SOUNDSCAPE

If you climb to the top of a hill and look down on the valley below, what you see is a landscape. But if you stop, sit down and listen—truly listen—you'll hear the **soundscape**. If you want to hear it in its natural state, you will need to be as gentle and quiet as possible. You may hear a chorus of singing birds, chattering rodents, buzzing insects, rustling leaves or the rippling sound of a river.

As you listen closely, try to distinguish three different types of sound. The **biophony** is the sound of living organisms. It includes the twittering of birdsong, the rhythmic chirping of field crickets, the throaty croaking of bullfrogs and the excited thrumming of cicadas from the treetops. The **geophony** is produced by nonliving elements—the whistling wind, the babbling brook, the pitter-patter of rainfall. These make up the underlying acoustic canvas upon which living organisms make their calls.

A young boy looks out over the glacier-fed waters of Moraine Lake in Banff National Park, AB. Sounds in the pristine mountain air travel long distances. Most people find the absence of anthrophony peaceful.
PAUL BIRIS/GETTY IMAGES

Half of all complaints about environmental pollution in Shanghai are about noise pollution. Street noise, including cultural and sporting events, is one of the biggest concerns for residents. JACZHOU/GETTY IMAGES

The sounds created by human activity are the third type of soundscape, the **anthrophony** (sometimes called anthropophony). Highway traffic, airplanes, cruise ships, personal watercraft, snowmobiles, drilling rigs and excavation machinery are all part of the anthrophony. Human noise is invading natural landscapes at an alarming rate all over the world. It is next to impossible to find any place on Earth that has not been affected by it. And if you do find a place, you have become the anthrophony yourself! The soundscape heard by a listener at any given location includes all three types of sound.

BIOACOUSTICS

Bioacoustics is the study of the communication between living things. It includes how sounds are made and how they are heard. Animal sounds cover a wide range of frequencies, often lower or higher than human ears can hear. The highest-frequency call in the animal world is that of the Ganges river dolphin, a blind freshwater dolphin that navigates using echolocation. Its clicks, bursts and twitters reach over 250 kHz, six octaves higher than the highest note on a typical piano.

A construction worker uses a jackhammer, one of the louder noises encountered in city life. A single jackhammer on cement reaches 100 to 120 decibels in intensity, a level that can cause immediate harm to the ears of someone passing by.
BRUCE EURKHARDT/GETTY IMAGES

Bucks let out a loud grunting sound when challenging other bucks.
JOHN DAVIDSON

While most animals vocalize during daylight hours, nocturnal animals such as coyotes, hyenas, badgers and bats choose to make their calls at night. Some birds and insects prefer an open, dry environment for vocalizing, while others choose to sing in wetland areas. A fellow biologist has noticed loons repeatedly calling near lakeshore cliffs, the echo off the rock faces prolonging and dramatizing the loon's haunting calls.

ACOUSTIC SIGNATURES

Every living thing has its own way of moving in time and space. Most species have a unique acoustic signature—a recognizable sequence of sounds of different frequencies. Using special acoustic sensors, researchers can hear the subtlest of sounds—even an earthworm as it wriggles through the soil.

Acoustic biologists often say that an organism such as an insect is "singing," but it's not like the singing of a person using their vocal cords. Animals, plants and insects can create sounds by rubbing body parts together, moving particles of earth or forcing air out of a number of possible passages. Birds sing their songs through a **syrinx**, while crickets rub their wings together. But they both chirp. Birders and ornithologists (bird scientists) have their own descriptive sound languages. For example, blackbirds make a *tchup,* evening grosbeaks a *krrr,* northern flickers a *kew* and dark-eyed juncos a soft *tew-tew-tew* call. The lyrebird has a call that sounds just like a laser gun (honestly)!

A library of terms exists to describe the sounds of life, but it is continuously changing. So as you listen closely to the biophony around you, can you come up with new words to describe their songs? Of course, you can even record the sounds to listen to them again later. Digital recorders have helped further the development of the relatively new discipline of **soundscape ecology**. Recordings of whole ecosystems are slowly becoming recognized as valuable tools to assess changes in ecosystems. For example,

SOUND BITE
A rattlesnake's tail is made of loose-fitting segments of keratin, the material in your fingernails. When the snake is startled, its tail muscles contract 50 to 100 times a second. The tail segments click together, creating the high-pitched rattle that can make your hair stand on end.

AMWU/DREAMSTIME.COM

recordings can be made in a forest before a logging operation. After the cutting is completed, new recordings can reveal how the native animal and bird populations have changed. Sound monitoring can be continued on a regular basis to determine how the forest biodiversity recovers. It's easier to place recording devices than to locate and count animals, especially birds, in dense forest ecosystems.

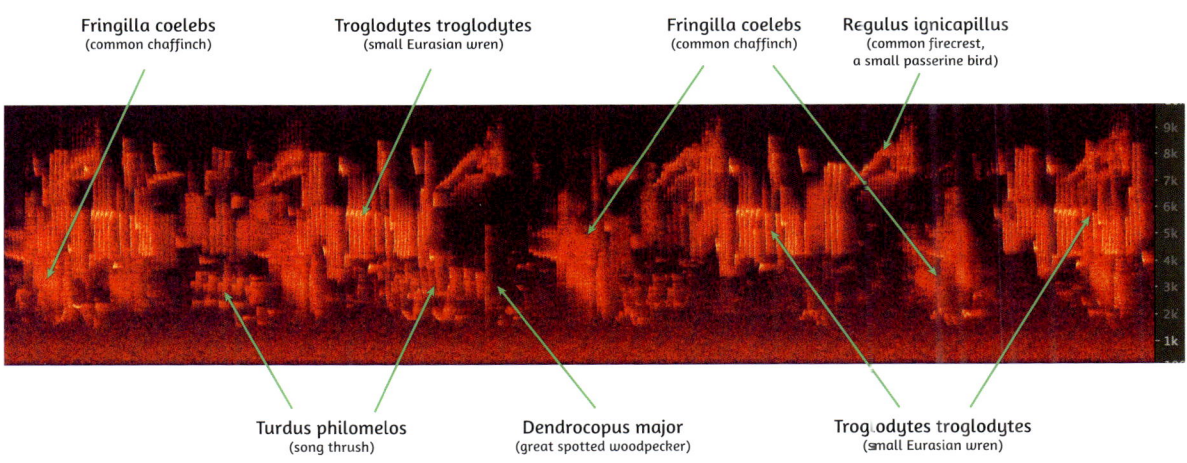

A spectrograph of a recording made in the Sasso Fratino rainforest in Italy.
PHOTO AND SPECIES IDENTIFICATION BY ALMO FARINA; ACOUSTIC FILES COURTESY OF GIANNI PAVAN. COMMON NAMES ADDED BY THE AUTHOR

Sound Research

If you visit some large sand dunes, you may hear them before you see them. Local folklore often attributes dune songs to ghosts or spirits living in the sand. But recently researchers with recording equipment have discovered the source of the dune songs. They found that a disturbance along the crest of the dune, either by wind, a person or an animal, creates small avalanches that roll down the slopes. The collective sound of the sand grains rolling over one another produces a unique sound that can often be heard for several miles.

It turns out that the frequency of the dune song varies with the size and shape of the individual grains of sand. Larger, heavier grains roll at a slower rate, producing a lower-frequency sound. Smaller, lighter grains roll more quickly. Of course, not all dunes have a song—but then again, not everyone can sing.

These two kids are enjoying the sand dunes in the Namib Desert, which contains some of the highest dunes in the world. Visitors claim it is so silent there that you can hear the geckos calling each other.
VINCENT BOISVERT/GETTY IMAGES

When plum-headed parakeets are happy, they sing, just like many people do in the shower. Parakeets learn about a thing by listening to the noises it makes.
© RHONDA HIMES

Crickets make their signature summer sound by rubbing their wings together (stridulating). The raised wings of this male cricket indicate that it is trying to attract females to mate with.
SIMON SHIM/SHUTTERSTOCK.COM

DEEP LISTENING

Have you ever been on a soundwalk? It's a walk in nature with the specific purpose of listening to natural sounds. Through deep listening we can learn a lot about the living organisms that surround us as well as the geophony, such as the wind blowing through the trees, the sound of the rain hitting the different leaf surfaces or the pattern of waves breaking on the shore of nearby bodies of water. Listen for the birds in your area. They may be quiet when you first enter—they can sense an intruder. But if you're gentle and patient, they will soon start singing again.

The high-pitched chirping of crickets and other insects contains a wealth of valuable information. The male cricket's chirps (stridulations) increase in speed as the air temperature rises and slow down when temperatures drop. You can calculate the air temperature in Fahrenheit degrees by counting the number of chirps in a 15-second period and then adding 37 (this number varies with the species). For example, three chirps a second means that it is 45+37=82°F (28°C). Crickets get more active when it's hot! So if you can't get to sleep on your camping trip, keep busy counting cricket chirps and figure out the temperature. It's much more fun than counting sheep!

NEIGHBORHOOD WATCH

Recent studies show that some animals eavesdrop on the neighborhood chatter before venturing out from the safety of their homes. If there is danger in the vicinity, chances are other animals are sounding the alarm.

In one study of gray squirrels, researchers broadcast a recording of the cry of a red-tailed hawk, a squirrel predator. The squirrels displayed "vigilance behavior"—freezing in midstride or standing straight up on their hind legs. When the researchers broadcast birdsong, an acoustic signal for a relaxed habitat, the squirrels emerged from their nests. This study shows that animals take environmental cues by listening to neighboring species, such as native birds, rodents that have common predators, or members of their own species. Diligent animals, like the squirrels in this study, can conserve energy by reducing anxiety. More time is available for collecting food, eating, and building nests, giving the animal a higher likelihood of survival. Sometimes consulting the "neighborhood watch" can mean the difference between life and death.

A gray squirrel in alert mode, listening for danger signals in the surrounding environment. Although squirrels don't have a language, they are known to be quite chatty. They communicate with each other and other species with a squawk-like call.
SZGABOR1987/SHUTTERSTOCK.COM

WHAT'S THAT NOISE?

The sound of human activity—anthrophony—has spread to almost every region of our planet. Cities are growing larger and louder. Farmland, which often borders on natural areas, is becoming increasingly noisy with tractors, diesel generators and other farm machinery. Oil rigs, quarry trucks, mining equipment and ventilation systems add to the **cacophony**. Road networks are rapidly spreading into once pristine natural areas. The problem is that human noise interferes with animals' ability to hear the environmental sounds around them, including sounds from members of their own species.

Ecologists have studied the impact of noise on bullfrogs. These amphibians are known to synchronize their calls into a chorus of sound—it's how they avoid being singled out by predators such as hawks. It's hard to pick out an individual voice in a loud, crowded room, and it's even more difficult in a swampy wetland. However, the noise from road traffic on nearby highways and air traffic overhead is interrupting the bullfrog chorus. This is giving hawks a chance to locate and prey on individual frogs, which may have long-term effects on bullfrog populations.

SOUND BITE

Male cicadas use a special sound-producing organ called a *tymbal* to make their shrill. Tiny abdominal muscles contract at speeds of several hundred times per second to produce this unique and powerful sound of summer.

Male cicadas make their sound by expanding and contracting the tymbal membrane in their abdomen. The hotter it gets, the louder the sound they make.
BECCA_ELLISON/GETTY IMAGES

What effect do other vehicles, like all-terrain vehicles (ATVs) and snowmobiles, have on the pristine Arctic environment or in our national parks? These are some of the areas of concern that sound ecologists and conservationists are investigating using the research tools of soundscape ecology.

A plane with tourists on safari lands in the savanna near grazing antelopes in a Tanzanian national park. The low drone of air traffic spreads far and wide in this open African environment.
GUDKOV ANDREY/SHUTTERSTOCK.COM

NATURAL MUSICIANS

Some musicians are highly sensitive to environmental sounds. But it's a rare musician or composer who can devote their entire life to creating nature-inspired music.

Raymond Murray Schafer is a Canadian composer who has long had nature as his muse. He coined the term *soundscape* when he started the World Soundscape Project (WSP), an educational, sound-research group at Simon Fraser University in British Columbia in the 1960s.

"In a way the world is a huge musical composition that is going on all the time without a beginning and presumably

A hydrophone is used to listen to and record sounds underwater. In deep, dark ocean waters, where visibility is low, sound takes on an even greater level of importance.
BY WILDESTANIMAL/GETTY IMAGES

without an ending," says Schafer. "We can improve it or we can destroy it. We can add more noises or we can add more beautiful sounds. It's up to us."

In the 1960s musician Bernie Krause became interested in the sounds of nature. He started investigating natural sounds to integrate into a studio album he was recording with his late music partner, Paul Beaver, in 1968. Krause was raised in the city, so at first he didn't like being alone in the wild. But sitting in the forest with a microphone and earphones, he found himself spellbound. He later went back to school to study bioacoustics and went on to become a founding father of the new discipline of soundscape ecology. Bernie and his wife, Kat, run Wild Sanctuary, which focuses on recording and archiving the sounds of wild places all over the world.

John Luther Adams is a Grammy-winning American composer. His music is inspired by the vast landscapes of Alaska. *The Place Where You Go to Listen*, his sound and light installation at University of Alaska Museum of the North, gives voice to the geophony. In a special listening room, speakers broadcast a continuous composition that is inspired by *and* powered by the cycles of daylight and darkness, the phases of the moon, vibrations in Earth's **mantle** and the northern lights.

The northern lights, or aurora borealis, light up the night sky in northern Canada. There are numerous reports of crackles and other sounds coming from the spectacular light displays. Scientists are studying the theory that the sounds are caused by electrical discharges in the air.
THIENTHONGTHAI WORACHAT/GETTY IMAGES

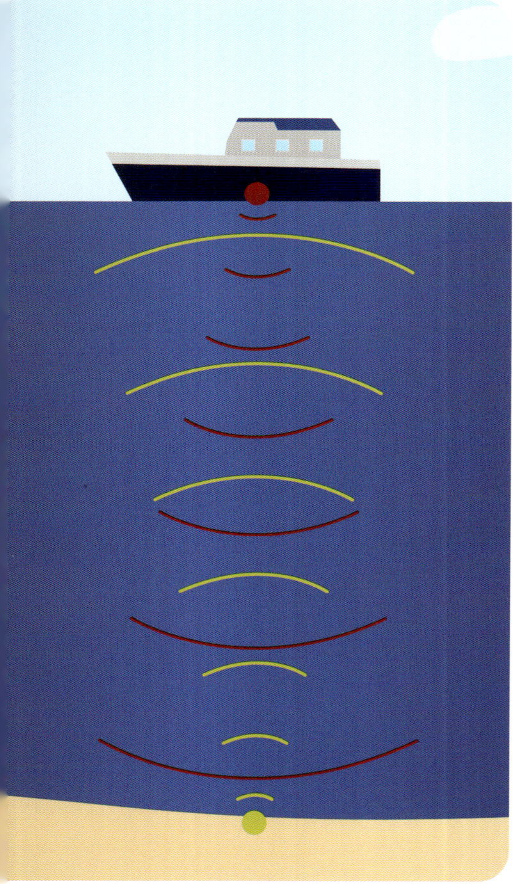

NOISE POLLUTION IN THE OCEAN

Fish have lived in our oceans for hundreds of millions of years, whales for about 50 million, and dolphins for over 10 million. These animals rely on noise-free waters to locate habitats, communicate over long distances, avoid predators, hunt prey and find mates. Noise in our oceans has doubled nearly every decade over the last two centuries. Cargo ships, cruise ships, barges, oil rigs and recreational vessels are increasing in number every year.

Underwater exploration for oil and gas often uses **seismic** explosions to help geologists map the ocean floor and discover fossil-fuel reserves. The extremely loud air-gun blasts are so powerful that the shock waves penetrate hundreds of miles into the earth's crust. Many animals are forced to flee their habitat to escape these intense sounds.

Sonar is another high-intensity sound that travels underwater for hundreds of miles. It is used worldwide to locate underwater vessels and find natural resources hidden under the ocean floor. But sonar can cause inner-ear damage in marine animals and interfere with the ability of whales and dolphins to navigate and communicate. Incidents of beaked whales ending up disoriented in shallow waters and stranded on beaches have been linked to naval sonar.

Sonar and seismic explosions can lead to an imbalance in predator/prey relationships as animals are forced to relocate to sound-free areas. Legislation limiting oceanic noise is urgently needed to protect our marine life. Increasing the number and size of marine protected areas (MPAs), which ban intense ocean noise, is a first step toward providing more places for species to take refuge.

Many studies have shown how noise is adversely impacting animals in their natural habitat. Scientists are also investigating the effect of city noise on the people who live there.

The illustration shows ultrasonic sound waves emitted by a ship's sonar transducer. The sound bounces off objects in the water and off the ocean floor and returns an "echo" to the ship. Sonar helps in locating submerged objects and mapping the seabed.
GRITSALAK KARALAK/SHUTTERSTOCK.COM

A beaked whale surfaces in ocean waters with an offshore oil rig in the background. Along with the danger of oil spills, marine biologists are studying the impact of underwater noise from the rigs on marine animals.
CHAKORN AMORNSET/SHUTTERSTOCK.COM

CHAPTER THREE

Sound Health

"Behold the new orchestra: the sonic universe! And the musicians: anyone and anything that sounds!"
—R. Murray Schafer, *The Soundscape: Our Sonic Environment and the Tuning of the World*

HEALING SOUNDS

Traditional Indigenous knowledge systems around the world are rich in examples of the health benefits of time spent in forests and other ecosystems.

Brain scans, heart-rate monitors and behavioral tests are now being used to study the *physiological* effects of exposure to nature. Early results show that natural sounds reduce the fight-or-flight response, lowering stress and anxiety, and increase participants' ability to relax, especially those people who came in with high stress levels. In hospital settings, even the presence of windows with views of nature and access to the sounds of wildlife can have positive effects on patients' ability to heal. When I was in the hospital recuperating from surgery after tumbling down a mountainside (not a recommended activity), I shifted from a windowless, artificially lit room to one with a view of a small park. My well-being and recovery were boosted immediately. I'm happy to say I now have 98 percent mobility in my shoulder.

The benefits of the ancient Japanese practice of shinrin-yoku, also known as forest bathing, have long been recognized. Medical scientists are now measuring the physiological effects.

Sometimes we don't realize how much noise is in our daily lives until we reach a place that is peaceful and quiet.
COMPASSIONATE EYE FOUNDATION/GETTY IMAGES

Trees and plants release healing essential oils, often in response to an injury to a leaf or stem, making the healing effects available to those in the surrounding area.

Nature-based therapies have proven effective in treating *post-traumatic stress disorder (PTSD)* in war veterans and victims of crime and accidents. Forest bathing has even helped working dogs traumatized in the line of duty.

NOISE!!!

What do aircraft, trains, trucks, cars, off-road vehicles, snowmobiles, personal watercraft, boats, container ships, factories, air conditioners, ventilation systems, compressor stations, excavation machinery, lawn mowers, leaf blowers, wood chippers and drilling rigs have in common? They produce noise—a lot of it! Studies show that people living in places with high noise levels (defined as an overabundance of chaotic, unwanted sound) have 15 percent more cases of anxiety and depression.

Among the many sources of noise pollution in cities, vehicle traffic is the most significant, especially on India's busy streets. Noise-control regulations are rarely enforced.
PETER ADAMS/GETTY IMAGES

> **SOUND BITE**
>
> During the COVID-19 pandemic many people reported that birds were singing louder. In fact, the birds only sounded louder because of the drop in background noise. Animals, like people, call and sing louder in a noisy environment, a response known as the *Lombard effect*.

In the United States, over three-quarters of all land is within one mile of a roadway. Noise causes birds and animals to change their behavior. Ecological soundscape studies show that natural areas invaded by traffic noise have 25 percent fewer visits by migrating birds.

During the COVID-19 lockdowns, an urban soundscape study showed that average noise levels dropped by 5 dBs in New York City. A separate study using seismographs (instruments that record vibrations in the earth's crust) revealed that reduced human activity during the pandemic led to a 50 percent drop in surface-level vibrations in populated areas—we humans do not tread lightly on this earth!

GETTING HEARD ABOVE THE DIN

Noise pollution affects the health and behavior of animals. Studies have noted several species of birds adjusting their calls to be heard above the din of anthrophony. The male great tit is a bird that increases the pitch of its call in an attempt to be heard above invasive noise. But females of the species prefer males with lower-frequency calls. Males with low-frequency songs are therefore placed in a difficult position—sing at their natural frequency and not be heard, or sing at a higher frequency and potentially be dismissed by the females. Tough call!

We often don't think about the impact of noise on our planet's smaller living organisms. Perhaps it's because insects are everywhere—they make up 80 percent of the world's species. Noisy environments could add to the list of threats facing many insect species. Safari ants, common in Kenya, often organize themselves into single, unbroken lines that snake across the ground. A typical ant colony, which can contain over 20 million ants, sends out expeditions in search of termites to bring back to their nests for forced labor. If the safari-ant lines are broken, either by strong winds, rain or the footsteps of

Bathers cool off on a hot summer day at Pensacola Beach, FL. During the COVID-19 pandemic, the level of human noise in the ocean was reduced by 20 percent in 2020. Ocean scientists reported that large marine mammals came closer to coastlines and waterways.
JIM MCKINLEY/GETTY IMAGES

One of the ways some ant species communicate while building their large nests is by rubbing hard sections of their abdomens together to make chirping sounds. IMGORTHAND/GETTY IMAGES

wayward travelers, the ants vigorously reorganize, despite the fact that they are all completely blind. How do they do it? They "sing"! Ecologists believe that the ants' humming sound, created by rubbing various body parts together, helps them reassemble their lines.

Bats have excellent hearing. Many bat species hunt by listening for the movement of insects on the ground. Studies from the natural-gas fields of New Mexico show that Brazilian free-tailed bats change their behavior in areas near the loud compressors that power some wells. The bats spend 40 percent less time in those areas. Some bats also narrowed the acoustic range of their calls near the machinery to separate their voices from the noise.

There is a growing body of research on the impacts of urban noise. Urban planners need to take these findings into consideration and design safer, quieter urban environments for our urban wildlife and for the people living there.

Canada geese are noisy visitors, making loud honks, barks, cackles and the occasional hiss. This gaggle of geese is walking along a bike path in Ottawa, Canada's capital, on a warm summer day.
RENATA APANAVICIENE/SHUTTERSTOCK.COM

Young students crowd into a primary-school classroom in Nkhotakota, Malawi. Packed in closely, without desks, many pupils will have difficulty hearing and paying attention to the teacher's words. DIETMAR TEMPS/SHUTTERSTOCK.COM

A young girl with protective headphones listens to music at the Castle Party dark independent festival in Bolków, Poland. Public events have become a large contributor to rising noise levels in cities around the world.
DZIUREK/SHUTTERSTOCK.COM

A streaked laughingthrush tries out its wings in an attempt to lift off. When juvenile birds leave the nest, their songs become an important means of communicating with other members of their species.
© RHONDA HIMES

NOISE AND THE DEVELOPING MIND

Developing young minds are particularly affected by noise. From daycare centers to classrooms for all ages, learning environments are highly vulnerable. Children under the age of 10 who are still learning basic language skills need to hear their teachers. Noise covers the subtle sounds required for learning languages, and learning difficulties at this stage can impede academic success later in life. It's worse for kids in poor school districts and in poor countries because they have higher student-teacher ratios and therefore (you guessed it) noisier classrooms.

Noise is not just created inside crowded classrooms—it can invade the learning environment from outside as well. Studies indicate that sounds from ventilation systems, machinery, construction equipment, airplanes, traffic and crowded sidewalks near schools can lead to lower academic performance. When it reaches stressful levels, noise can contribute to sleep disturbances and mental-health issues in students. Noisy environments are particularly harmful for children with autism and those with attention deficit disorder (ADD).

According to one study, zebra finch juveniles (teenagers in the bird world) that grow up with high levels of city noise have shorter life spans than those brought up in natural environments. Some bird species inherit all their bird songs (through their genetic makeup), but others learn their songs from their parents. Environmental noise can impede this learning process, just as it does in humans.

ULTRA AND INFRA SOUNDS

As you read in chapter 1, humans hear sounds with a frequency between 20 Hz and 20,000 Hz (20 kHz). *Ultrasound* refers to those sounds that are above 20 kHz. Many animals, like bats, hear and communicate in this range. They use high-pitched calls to navigate during their high-speed aerobatics. The underwater version of ultrasound, sometimes called *biosonar*, is used by orcas and dolphins to navigate, communicate, hunt and perform spectacular aquatic maneuvers.

Sounds below 20 Hz are *infrasound*. Some geophony, such as the rumble of earthquakes or volcanoes, falls into the infrasound range (think the lowest note on a church pipe organ). Elephants, rhinos, hippos and alligators don't perform bat-like aerobatics, but they do use infrasound to communicate over some incredibly long distances—hundreds of miles in the case of whales. That in itself is pretty spectacular. But in remote regions, infrasound from coal mining, industrial processes, railways, wind turbines and transport trucks is interfering with the interactions between animals that communicate in this frequency range.

> **SOUND BITE**
> Dolphins hear through their teeth—no wonder they always appear to be smiling. The dolphin's "dental antennae" and lower jawbone act as sound receivers, allowing the cetacean to create a sound map to navigate through its environment.

Human ears can hear frequencies between 20 Hz and 20 kHz. Infrasound frequencies—those below 20 Hz—are heard by some animals, including elephants. The ultrasound range—frequencies above 20 kHz—is heard by cats and dogs, up to 40 kHz. Dolphins and bats hear frequencies up to 160 kHz.

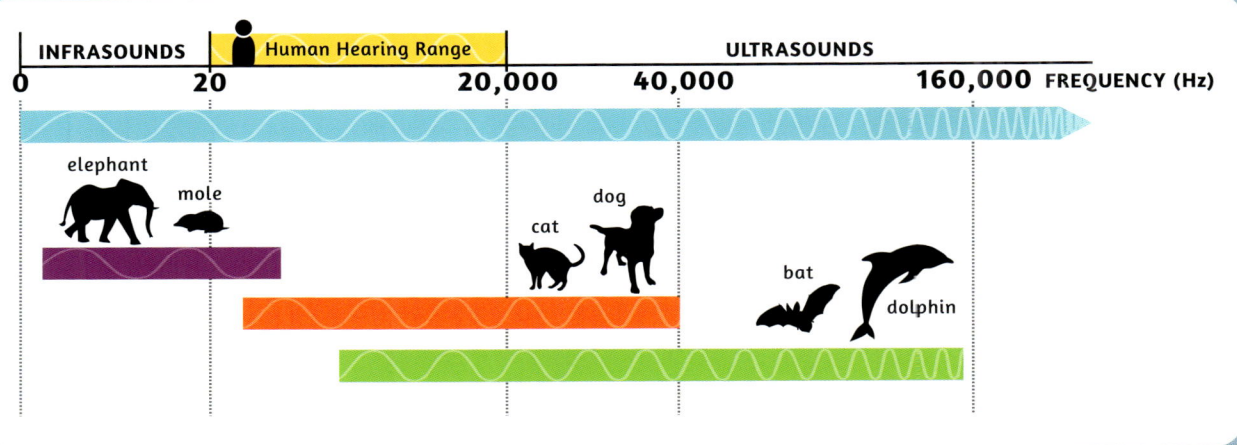

Sound Research

Tarsiers, buggy-eyed tree-dwellers from the Philippines, are the only primates that communicate in pure ultrasound. The tarsier's open-mouthed, wide-eyed gaze was long thought to be a type of yawn. However, recent recordings made with ultrasound detectors have revealed that the animals are actually emitting a high-pitched, open-mouthed call too high to be heard by human ears. The natural frequency of their call is 70 kHz, one of the highest ever recorded for a land-based mammal. This private, high-pitched channel could allow the tiny primates to alert each other to the presence of insects, snakes, lizards and predatorial birds. The discovery has scientists wondering how many other open-mouthed animals might also be sending ultrasonic calls.

Audible sounds from tarsiers include high-pitched squeaks and squeals, often heard at dawn, as they leave their roosting sites, and at dusk, when they return.
VITALY TITOV/DREAMSTIME.COM

THE POWER OF SOUND

Acoustic weapons have been used between enemies for thousands of years. The trumpet blasts of priests in the Israelite army helped in the storming of Jericho 3,500 years ago. Long-range acoustic devices blasted at 150 dBs are a form of naval defense, deterring smaller boats from approaching naval ships. In a new solution to an old problem, cruise ships sailing around the Horn of Africa have used these devices to drive away pirate ships.

Animals also use sound as a weapon. They stun and sometimes kill prey with their powerful sounds. The force of a Bengal tiger's roar when it attacks reportedly leaves victims feeling completely stunned and defenseless. Then there's the pistol shrimp, which has an "open carry" license. Its weapon? An enormous enlarged claw with a super speedy underwater snap shoots bubble bullets at close to 62 miles per hour (100 kilometers per hour). The sound of the **cavitation** bubbles collapsing from seawater pressure creates a shock wave powerful enough to kill marine worms, crabs and small fish swimming nearby. In fact,

A Bengal tiger bares its powerful canine teeth and lets out a full-throated roar. But when engaged in a fight, these tigers don't roar—they hiss and fluff at their opponents.
SETTA SORNNOI/SHUTTERSTOCK.COM

pistol shrimp have to keep a safe distance from each other or risk getting caught in accidental friendly fire.

An organism's size is not the sole determinant of the power of its sound. Animals in a colony can make their defense more convincing by synchronizing their calls. A rice-sized shrimp does just that! This sponge dweller protects its home against potential intruders by rhythmically snapping its claws. The simple signal inspires other shrimp in the colony to join in and snap along to the same beat. The result is a loud message to all marauders—keep out!

The Pink Floyd pistol shrimp, a species of snapping shrimp, was named after the rock band Pink Floyd in part because it has a distinctive bright pink-red claw. The sound of the snapping claw reaches 210 dBs, intense enough to kill nearby small fish.
ARTHUR ANKER/WIKIMEDIA COMMONS/CC BY-SA 4.0

LEARNING FROM NATURE

Nature is incredibly creative. Inventors in the fields of robotics, medicine, engineering and architecture have often turned to the natural world for inspiration. At the University of Toronto, attention is on a tiny yellow parasitic fly that lays its larvae on male crickets. (The larvae burrow into the crickets to grow, killing them as they emerge.) The fly has remarkable hearing and is able to determine the exact location of the sounds it hears. A time-delay mechanism allows the nocturnal fly to locate the chirps of male crickets and deposit its eggs accurately in the dark. The fly's two eardrums are joined together inside—possible since its ears are only 0.08 inches (2 millimeters) apart. The vibrations activating one eardrum push on the eardrum in the other ear. The minuscule amount of time required to activate the second eardrum is enough for the fly to determine the exact direction of the incoming sound. Medical researchers have used this discovery to develop an entirely new generation of direction-sensitive microphones used in hearing aids.

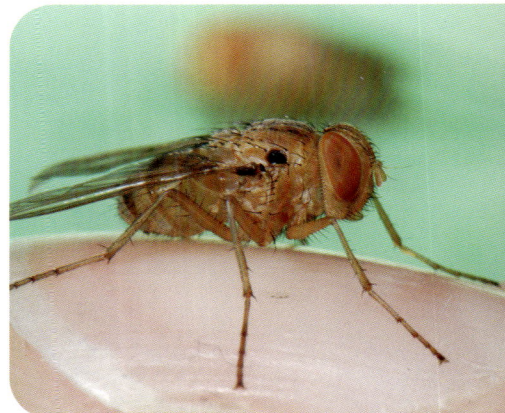

A female yellow parasitic fly, Ormia ochracea, *rests on a fingernail. This tiny fly's directional hearing is unique in the animal kingdom.*
JPAUR/WIKIMEDIA COMMONS/CC BY-SA 3.0

SOUND BITE
A rainforest cricket species has the highest-frequency call of any insect. Its secret? Highly efficient elastic energy. A special scraper on one wing gets wedged and distorted on a series of pegs on the other wing and then springs back. At superfast wing-beat speeds, this creates a high-pitched sound of 130 kHz.

Many people who meditate regularly report an increase in their attention span and in their ability to listen to their environment.
JUSTIN PAGET/GETTY IMAGES

THE SEARCH FOR SILENCE

Stop right now and listen. What do you hear? The refrigerator? Traffic? The hum of your computer? The sound of the furnace or air conditioner? Even if you are out in nature, chances are you'll hear the distant hum of road or air traffic. We are surrounded by noise!

Is there any land area that is completely silent? Antarctica comes to mind. It has no permanent residents and only a few thousand people (scientists and support staff) on a land area of over 5.41 million square miles (14 million square kilometers). That should be quiet, right? Wrong! Even in Antarctica, along with the natural geophony and biophony, you'll hear the rumbling of planes roaming the skies, the engine noise of offshore research boats and the roar of diesel generators powering living quarters and laboratories. In the cold, dry environment of Antarctica there is nothing to absorb those sounds, so they reverberate over very long distances.

A NASA research plane surveys mountain glaciers in Alaska. As the Arctic Ocean becomes ice-free for longer periods each year, there's noise from more and more planes and ocean vessels reverberating through the crisp Arctic air.
NASA/CHRIS LARSEN, UNIVERSITY OF ALASKA-FAIRBANKS

My niece Sarah is a biologist with Parks Canada in the far north. She told me that she was attracted to the Arctic region while doing her master's research in ornithology (the study of birds) because of the gentle quiet of the landscape. But the high north is not the peaceful refuge it used to be. It is now directly under the flight paths of international passenger planes en route from North America to Europe and Asia.

Perhaps a silent environment is not really what we want. After all, life is noisy. But we share this planet with many other species, and human noise should not threaten their existence. The soundscapes of our natural places need to be cherished and conserved—they are a vital part of the earth's natural heritage, and the caretaking responsibility has fallen to us.

Sound Research

Owls rely on stealth, not speed. Sharp vision and excellent hearing are key to their nighttime hunts. From their perches, owls use their agile ears to locate the source of even the slightest sound. So how do these large raptors remain so quiet in the night sky? It turns out it's all in the design!

Owl wings are broader than most birds', giving them more uplift and keeping them afloat in the air. Compared to other predatory birds, like falcons, owls need fewer flaps to cover the same distances. Falcon wings are slick and crisp at the edges, and they slice through the air like an arrow at speeds of 200 miles per hour (322 kilometers per hour). But there is a loud swoosh that accompanies the flight. Owl feathers are custom-designed for silence. A comblike serrated edge with tiny, hooked barbs breaks the wind and reduces air turbulence during dives. The feathers on the wing's trailing edge are soft, giving the bird an additional silent advantage over its prey. The overall look of the owl's body is soft and fuzzy, making it a flying sound blanket—and for the prey, it's a deadly silence.

A barn owl in flight prepares for a landing. Dawn and dusk are owls' favorite times of day to hunt. Their acute sense of hearing helps them locate small mammals on the ground below.
MZPHOTO.CZ/SHUTTERSTOCK.COM

CHAPTER FOUR

Conserving Natural Sounds

"Those who contemplate the beauty of the earth find reserves of strength that will endure as long as life lasts."
—Rachel Carson

THE ART OF LISTENING

The loss of animal and plant species on the earth is occurring faster than ever. Global population studies estimate there will be over nine billion people by 2050. Our survival depends on how we learn to live with the estimated eight million different species with whom we share the planet. Environmental sound recordings can be used to study change and monitor the effects of human activity on the natural world. The earlier we can hear change, the quicker we can act to avert potential disasters such as loss of species. Animals have been using the art of listening to survive for millennia.

Through evolution, prey animals have developed mechanisms to avoid their predators. Sound has played its role. For instance, bats are the biggest threat to several moth species. A particular species of tiger moth has evolved a high-pitched, rhythmic clicking, produced by rubbing various body parts together. This disrupts the echolocation mechanism bats use to hunt their prey,

A garden tiger moth rests on a lichen-covered rock. The bright colors are a warning to predators that the moths are distasteful. The tiger moth can rub its wings together and make a rasp-like sound.
MIKE POWLES/GETTY IMAGES

A young girl sits quietly, eyes closed, at the base of a tree, listening to the sounds of the forest. Every time you try this exercise, you will find your ability to attend the sounds around you gets stronger.
WESTEND61/GETTY IMAGES

causing them to miss their targets. The moths have learned to stay one step ahead of the bats by jamming their radar.

So how can we train our ears to hear subtle auditory cues in nature? With a good understanding of the natural sonic environment, we can better detect the warning signals that human actions are about to cause habitats to go out of balance. Only then can conservation plans be developed to restore the natural setting and reduce the impact of human activities.

Try this! Find a broad tree for a back rest in a natural area as free from urban noise as safely possible. Make sure you can sit comfortably. This is your "sit spot." Close your eyes and clear your mind. I like to close my ears too, using my index finger to block my ear canals for 15 to 20 seconds. Now just listen from your seat in nature's symphony hall. Slowly, as your own nervous system becomes still, you will be able to tune in to the richness of the soundscape. You will start to hear some of the individual animal calls near you. Then try to listen to sounds farther and farther away. Keep doubling the size of your listening circle. You will be surprised how far you can hear. Soon you will remain alert to the soundscape every time you're out in nature.

SOUND BITE

The blue whale, the largest animal known to exist on Earth (its tongue alone is as heavy as an elephant), has one of nature's loudest calls. It can hear other blue whales that are as far away as 1,000 miles (1,600 kilometers).

Sound Research

Dolphins are "wake hunters." They follow boats, scooping up disoriented fish trapped by the pressure waves in the boat's wake. Frightened and confused land animals fleeing an unexpected intruder in their habitat are also vulnerable to wake hunting. Hawks have been observed hunting in pairs—the first hawk swoops in, often making loud attack calls, and the second hawk follows in its wake, picking off startled victims.

The Presidio, a popular nature preserve in San Francisco, is made up of a mix of local wildlife and active urban dwellers. Some of the animals have adapted their hunting methods to urban living. Joggers running through the Presidio often startle birds and other animals, flushing them out of the bushes. Sharp-shinned hawks take advantage of the jogger's "wake," swooping in and grabbing the vulnerable prey. Biologists have also noted hawks using the loud noise created by passing aircraft or other vehicles to mask their attacks.

Hawk: A juvenile sharp-shinned hawk in flight. The typical alarm call is an excited kik-kik-kik. *Interestingly, the males are smaller in size and have higher voices than the females. Trees: Young kids run through a forest near Mount Alyeska in Girdwood, AK.*
HAWK: AGAMI PHOTO AGENCY/SHUTTERSTOCK.COM
TREES: IMAGE SOURCE TRADING LTD/SHUTTERSTOCK.COM

RECORDING IN NATURE

The ability to record the sounds around us has come a long way since the invention of the phonautograph over 160 years ago. Advances in digital sound recorders in the last 15 years have allowed for broad-spectrum nature recordings at a relatively cheap price. What's more, they are compact and quiet, making it possible to now hear some of the remotest places on Earth.

Whether animals are in a flock, herd, pack, swarm or team, they rely on hearing each other to increase their chances of survival. A danger call from one rodent will create vigilance in others, just like a cry for help does in our neighborhoods. Birds and other animals make calls for many other reasons too—to contact companions, aggressively expand territory, defend their habitat or, in the case of young birds, beg for food.

By making your own recordings, you can replay and study the sounds, eventually coming to know the difference between

Recordings of changes in the chorus of songbirds at dusk and at dawn can help researchers determine ecosystem impacts.
© LEONARD MODDERMAN AND RHONDA HIMES

various calls. However, it is important not to disturb the living species in the environment where you record. Also, less disturbance means more natural (i.e., better) recordings. Your files may one day provide data useful for scientific research or for environmental community events that mobilize people to act on important issues like climate change and habitat destruction.

ACOUSTIC MONITORING

Sounds are all around us, but rarely do we get a chance to "see" them. That's where the **spectrogram** comes in. It's a visual display of sounds, representing the intensity and frequency of sounds over time. Spectrograms help scientists analyze sound recordings.

Counting individual animals by visual means is an expensive, laborious process. Animals tend to modify their behavior in the

Advances in digital recorders, such as the one shown here on a small tripod, can help scientists hear what sometimes is difficult to see. Soundscape studies can be made by placing recorders throughout an entire habitat.
STEPHEN AITKEN

presence of human monitors, so accurate results are difficult. Soundscape studies on a landscape scale are now affordable and easier—an entire landscape can be monitored with digital recorders while collecting much more data than human observation can. The recordings can later be compared with others made at the same time of day, place and season.

Papua New Guinea is considered a healthy, species-rich habitat. It is the second-largest island in the world and a biodiversity hotspot, containing 5 to 10 percent of the world's species. Most of the frequencies in the soundscape are those of animal and insect sounds. Degraded landscapes, on the other hand, those that have been affected by human activities such as logging or mining, often have more noise and less variety in the frequencies of the biophony, indicating fewer species than landscapes in their natural state. Soundscape ecologists are testing the theory that a habitat with a sound spectrum filled with biological sounds—a sound spectrum in which most of the frequencies are occupied by the sounds of living organisms—is a biodiversity-rich, healthy habitat.

The Bismarck Archipelago in Papua New Guinea. The sound environment in this tropical rainforest is rich with the calls of a wide range of insects and animals. MARC DOZIER/GETTY IMAGES

THE SOUND OF CHANGE

Global warming changes ecosystems, though it may not be visually apparent on a daily or even a monthly basis. Sound recordings can be an effective way to monitor the changes. Higher temperatures and drier air tend to reduce plant density and increase droughts, resulting in more reverberation (or echo) in the sonic environment. These changes may make it difficult for some species to hear and communicate with each other. Have you ever tried to talk to your friends in a noisy cafeteria? Not all animals are able to adapt easily. Mating calls will most certainly be affected by acoustic changes. Will it benefit those hunting their prey or the prey themselves? Will these changes upset ecosystem balance? Will it result in some species relocating or dying out entirely? These are some of the questions conservationists and climatologists are considering.

What about the trees? David George Haskell, a biology professor in Tennessee, listens to trees. He believes that different species of trees have their own distinct voices. When wind blows through the branches and leaves of a tree, it responds by vibrating and shaking. A pine tree sounds different in the wind than an oak tree. A poplar, with its broad wobbly leaves, has a very different wind song than a spruce tree with short stout needles. Every tree has its own resonant sound and its own rain song, the sound of raindrops falling on its leaves, and branches. The enchantment created by the whispering of trees is so widespread that a word has been invented for it, *psithurism* (pronounced sith-err-iz-um), from the Greek word for whispering.

Birds are very choosy about the trees in which they nest and feed. They too become players in the tree's song and in the local soundscape. As a performance hall needs to maintain the high quality of sound in its theater, natural ecosystems also need to maintain their natural quality of sound. This will ensure that the species living there are able to communicate among themselves as they have done for thousands of years.

View of barren land following a fire near Kamloops, BC. Climate change increases the risk of hot, dry weather and other extreme weather events. Lightning strikes and strong winds add to the risk of more frequent and larger forest fires.
TOMS AUZINS/SHUTTERSTOCK.COM

EXPERT ADVICE

Once you or your friends have managed to make a recording in the wild, bring the memory card home and load it into a computer. When you click on the audio files, how do you know what you are listening to? Spectrograms generated by sound-editing software can be sent along with small sound files to willing bird and animal experts. Entomologists also get very excited about anyone interested in the insects they have spent their lives studying. To get started, here are some links to sites containing the soundscapes of a wide variety of ecosystems.

centerforglobalsoundscapes.org

The Center for Global Soundscapes at Purdue University has some wonderful programs, including summer camps on soundscape ecology. An enhanced program for kids who are visually challenged builds on their natural auditory strengths and trains participants to use these skills in soundscape studies and other STEM subjects.

recordtheearth.org

Join researchers to help map out the sounds of the planet and listen to the calls of the world's living organisms. This project, developed at Purdue University, has a downloadable app so that you can participate in recording the biophony, geophony and anthrophony. Their IMAX film, Global Soundscapes, takes you on an ear-opening journey into the science of sound. Visit soundscapeshow.com.

wildambience.com

Close your eyes, open your ears and listen to professional recordings on this site from the rainforests of Borneo, the arid Wyperfeld National Park in Australia or the mountain streams of the Himalayas.

wildsanctuary.com

Wild Sanctuary is the website of Bernie and Kat Krause. They offer audio recordings of wild places—you can hear the sounds of different habitats with the click of your cursor.

A young girl with a digital recorder, headphones and an external microphone. The windscreen is placed over the microphone to reduce intrusive noise from wind. YAORUSHENG/GETTY IMAGES

CONSERVATION OF NATURAL SOUNDSCAPES

Rachel Carson, in her 1962 book *Silent Spring*, was the first scientist to make the broader public aware of the dangers of environmental poisoning and a world in which all life has been silenced, a world devoid of bird, amphibian and insect songs. The threat at that time was the widespread use of the pesticide **DDT**.

Conservationists are now more aware that changes in the sonic environment of a habitat are a warning sign that might signal loss of species or severe changes in animal behavior. National parks, nature reserves and marine protected areas must develop soundscape conservation plans that recognize the impact of unwanted noise.

Twenty years ago, Zion National Park in Utah came up with a plan to deal with the traffic noise affecting both park wildlife and the visitor experience. Park managers started a shuttle service that allowed visitors to leave their cars behind and take a bus to the trailheads. The result? A quieter park and, as it turns out, more wildlife sightings. Now, as the shuttle fleet ages out, the gas-powered buses are being replaced with electric vehicles that are much quieter *and* carbon-free.

Expanding road networks, motorized watercraft, aircraft, snowmobiles and all-terrain vehicles operating near and within protected areas all threaten the ability of animals to communicate. Additional pressure on the soundscape comes from an ever-increasing number of visitors, invasion by domestic animals and development on land adjacent to these reserves. Soundscape workshops and education are needed to increase awareness of how to reduce the impact of the noise of human activity on the natural world.

Researchers at Rocky Mountain National Park in Colorado studied the park's acoustic environment extensively using recording equipment. In consultation with soundscape ecologists, they were able to determine the sources of invasive sounds,

A young girl peers up into the forest canopy while listening to the sounds of animal life resonating through the forest.
STOCKSTUDIOX/GETTY IMAGES

> **SOUND BITE**
> Small does not mean less powerful! The wren has one of the loudest calls of all the songbirds when measured on a per-ounce basis. It also has one of the longest songs—lasting up to 10 seconds per round. A high-energy diet of insects and spiders fuels its enthusiasm.

leading to a ban on low-flying aircraft over the park. After park staff educated the Federal Aviation Administration (FAA) on the impact of commercial flights in the park, the FAA changed some flight paths and landing procedures. The result was a more natural park experience for both visitors and the wildlife.

We share our planet with millions of other species. The first step in protecting them is to listen to what they have to say!

JOIN THE CONSERVATION CONVERSATION

The greatest thing you can do to help in the conservation of soundscapes is to fine-tune your ability to listen. Listen to the sounds of wildlife around you and discover their hidden messages. Did you know that the dawn bird chorus is louder than the evening chorus? Researchers say this is because the birds are tuning up their voices in the morning to prepare for a day of singing—not unlike professional opera singers preparing their performance voices.

Studies show that bird populations start to decline within a mile of a roadway. Road noise impairs their ability to communicate with one another by overpowering their calls. We must tell the people who design roads and vehicles, and the people who make and enforce our environmental laws, to consider the impact of anthrophony on our wild areas.

Stand up and let your voice be heard! Think of the birds that need quiet places to land during their migrations, the insects that need to hear other members of their swarm, and the primates, mammals, fish and rodents that need healthy sound environments in order to survive. As responsible neighbors of those whose voices are being silenced, we need not only to listen up but to speak up for them too!

Millaa Millaa Falls, in the Atherton Tablelands of North Queensland, Australia. This beautiful habitat is rich in both aquatic and terrestrial biodiversity.
ROBIN SMITH/GETTY IMAGES

Resources

Print

Clinton, Chelsea. *Start Now! You Can Make a Difference.* Puffin Books, 2020.

Edwards, Roberta. *Who Is Jane Goodall?* Grosset & Dunlap, 2012.

Fabiny, Sarah. *Who Was Rachel Carson?* Grosset & Dunlap, 2014.

Ignotofsky, Rachel. *The Wondrous Workings of Planet Earth: Understanding Our World and Its Ecosystems.* Ten Speed Press, 2018.

Krause, Bernie. *The Great Animal Orchestra: Finding the Origins of Music in the World's Wild Places.* Little, Brown and Company, 2012.

Thompson, Laurie Ann. *Be a Changemaker: How to Start Something That Matters.* Simon Pulse/Beyond Words, 2014.

Young, Jon. *What the Robin Knows: How Birds Reveal the Secrets of the Natural World.* Mariner Books, illustrated edition, 2013.

Online

ABC Kids Listen: abc.net.au/kidslisten/noisy-by-nature

Biodiversity Conservancy International: biodiversityconservancy.org

Bioneers: bioneers.org

Explore Sound, Acoustical Society of America: exploresound.org/educators-2/acoustics-lesson-plans

John Luther Adams: johnlutheradams.net

National Parks Service: nps.gov/subjects/sound/teaching.htm

Nature Soundmap: naturesoundmap.com

Rachel Carson: rachelcarson.org

Wild Ambience: wildambience.com

Wild Sanctuary: wildsanctuary.com

Links to external resources are for personal and/or educational use only and are provided in good faith without any express or implied warranty. There is no guarantee given as to the accuracy or currency of any individual item. The author and publisher provide links as a service to readers. This does not imply any endorsement by the author or publisher of any of the content accessed through these links.

Glossary

amplify—increase the volume of sound

anthrophony—sounds of human activity, sometimes referred to as *noise*

Big Bang theory—the leading explanation of how the universe began: a single point exploding into a continuous expansion, creating the billions of galaxies in our universe

bioacoustics—the study of sounds created and received by living organisms

biophony—sounds created by the activity of living organisms

biosonar—high-frequency sounds used by marine animals for navigation and communication

cacophony—a harsh, chaotic mixture of sound frequencies

cavitation—a vacuum formed in a liquid by a fast-moving body or high-intensity sound waves

cochlea—a spiral tube in the inner ear, shaped like a snail shell, containing the sensory organ of hearing

cosmic microwave background—electromagnetic radiation left over from the Big Bang in the form of microwaves that now fill the universe

DDT—(Dichloro-Diphenyl-Trichloroethane) the first human-made insecticide, now largely banned due to human and environmental health concerns

decibel—a unit measure of the intensity of a sound wave

echolocation—a technique used by animals to locate objects and navigate using high-frequency sound waves

frequency—the number of times a sound wave repeats itself per second; also known as *pitch*

geophony—sounds made by nonliving things in the environment; earth sounds

habitat—the natural home of an animal, plant or other organism

infrasound—sound vibrations that occur at frequencies below 20 Hz, inaudible to humans

invertebrates—multicellular animals with no backbones (or vertebrae)

Lombard effect—the tendency of animals and people to talk, call or sing louder in a noisy environment

mantle—the layer between Earth's superheated core and its outer crust. It makes up 84 percent of Earth's total volume.

phonautograph—the earliest known device for recording sound waves in the air

physiological—relating to the way that living organisms and their systems work

post-traumatic stress disorder (PTSD)—a mental-health disorder that can occur after someone experiences or witnesses a terrifying event

respiratory systems—systems of organs by which animals exchange gases with their environment, taking in oxygen and letting out carbon dioxide

seismic—caused by an earthquake, meteorite or other large vibration in the earth

sonar—an echolocation device used for finding underwater vessels or natural resources in marine environments

sonic boom—the loud clap heard when an object reaches or exceeds the speed of sound

soundscape—the audible sounds in an environment

soundscape ecology—the study of sound in the environment and how it impacts animals, plants, humans and ecological processes

spectrogram—a visual representation of sound waves, showing the strength of the various frequencies over a period of time

stridulate—make shrill, high-pitched sounds by rubbing body parts together; typical of insects

syrinx—the voice organ in almost all birds, situated in the lower larynx

terrestrial—relating to the land as distinct from air or water

tymbal—the vibrating membrane in a male cicada that produces its shrill

ultrasonic—having a frequency above the top range of human hearing

ultrasound—sound vibrations emitted at frequencies above 20 kHz

vacuum—a space with no matter in it, not even air

Index

Page numbers in **bold** *indicate an image caption.*

acoustic monitoring, 18–19, 36, 39–41
acoustic sensors, 18
Adams, John Luther, 23
aircraft, 9, **22**, **34**, 44
alligators, 9, 31
animal behaviors: alarm signals, 20–21, 38; hunting, 32–33, 38; impact of noise, 21–22, 29; mating calls, **20**, 41. *See also* communication
Antarctica, 34
anthrophony: defined, 17, 46; impact of, 21–22, 28. *See also* noise pollution
ants, 6, 28–29
aquatic sounds: and marine life, 9, 13, 24, 31; and noise pollution, 24, **28**; use of hydrophones, **22**
Arctic habitat, 22, **34**, 35

Banff National Park, Alberta, **16**
barn owl, **35**
bats, 10, 18, 29, 31, 36–37
beaked whale, 14, 24, **25**
Bell, Alexander Graham, 14–15
Bengal tiger, **32**
Big Bang theory, 8–9, 46
bioacoustics, 17–18, 46
biophony, 16, 18–19, 40, 46
biosonar, 31, 46
birds: behaviors, 18, 20, 28, **29**; ear structure, 12; loss of habitat, 28, 41; predators, 35, 38; songs of, 28, 30, **39**, 44; syrinx of, 18, 47
blackbirds, **2**
blue whale, 37
bullfrogs, 21

Canada geese, **29**
Carson, Rachel, 43
cats, 12, **31**, **32**

cell phones, 15
Center for Global Soundscapes, 42
children and learning, 14, 30
chimpanzees, 14
cicadas, 6, 21
communication: aquatic, 13, 24; bioacoustics, 17–18, 46; frequencies of, 9, 31; ground vibrations, 10; language, 13, 14; mechanisms, 6–7, 10, 18–19
conservation: and acoustic monitoring, 18–19, 36, 39–41; make your own recordings, 38–39; resources, 42, 45
Cooper, Martin, 15
cosmic microwave background, 8–9, 46
COVID-19 pandemic, 28
Cramer, John, 8
crickets, 6, 16, 18, 20, **33**

decibels (dBs), 9, 31, 46
deer, 7
digital sound recorders, **6**, 18–19, 38–39, **40**, **42**
dogs, 8–9, 12, 27, **31**
dolphins, 6, 9, 17, 24, 31, 38

ear structures, 11, 12, 33
earthworms, 18
echolocation, 10, 17, 36–37, 46
ecosystems. *See* habitats
Edison, Thomas, 14
elephants, 10, 31
emerald jumping spider, **10**

falcons, 35
Fessenden, Reginald, 15
finch, 30
fish, 6, 9, 13, 24, 38
flies, 33

forest habitat, 18, 37, 41
frequency (sound waves), 8, 9, 31, 46

Gagliano, Monica, 13
Ganges river dolphin, 17
geese, **29**
geophony: defined, 16, 46; infrasound, 31; listening to, 20, 23; sand dunes, 19; seismic, 24, 47
giraffes, 9
Goodall, Jane, 14
gray squirrel, 20–21
great tit, 28
ground vibrations, 10, 28

habitats: changes to, 21–22, 37, 40; defined, 46
hares, 12
Haskell, David George, 41
hawks, 38
health: meditation, **34**; and nature, 26–27; reduced stress, 26–27, 30
hearing mechanisms: ear structure, 11, 12, 33; skull bones, 12, 13, 31
howler monkey, 7
human activity: aircraft, 9, **22**, **34**, 44; during COVID-19, 28; increase in, 15, 17; oil industry, 24, **25**, 29; pesticide use, 43; roadways, 21, 28, 44; shipping, 24, 32; urban noise, **17**, 27–28, 29; uses of sound, 32. *See also* noise pollution
human hearing: damage to, 9, **17**; ear structure, 11; hearing aids, 33; range of, 9, 31

Indigenous knowledge, 26
infrasound, 31, 46
insects: sounds of, 6, 18, 20, 28; study of, 42
invertebrates, 6, 46

Krause, Bernie and Kat, 23, 42

language, 13, 14
laughingthrush, **30**
Lombard effect, 28, 46
loons, 18

Malawi, education in, **30**
marine life: communication, 9, 13, 24, 31; and noise pollution, 24, **28**
marine protected areas (MPAs), 24, 43
monkeys, 7
moths, 36

nature: and healing, 26–27; listening to, 20, 37, 44; and music, 23
New York City, 28
noise pollution: and human health, 27, 30; increase in, 7, 15, 17, 34–35; loss of species, 36, 40, 44; and wildlife, 7, 21–22, 31, 40. *See also* human activity
northern lights, 23

O'Connell, Caitlin, 10
oil industry, 24, **25**, 29
orcas, 31
owls, 12, 35

Papua New Guinea, 40
parakeets, **20**
parks and preserves, **16**, **22**, 38, 43–44
phonautograph, 14, 38, 47
pistol shrimp, 32–33
plants: and locating water, 13; sounds of, 6–7, 12–13, 41
plum-headed parakeet, **20**
predators, tactics of, 32–33, 35, 38
Presidio, San Francisco, 38
primates, 7, 9, 14, 32

protected areas: marine, 24, 43; parks and preserves, 22, 38, 43–44

rabbits and hares, 12
rattlesnakes, 18
red-winged blackbird, **2**
resources, 42, 45
road noise, 21, 28, 44
Rocky Mountain National Park (Colorado), 43–44

safari ants, 28–29
Schafer, Raymond Murray, 22–23
schools, and noise, 30
Scott de Martinville, Édouard-Léon, 14
seismic vibrations, 24, 47
Shanghai, **17**
sharks, 13
shipping activity, 24, 32
shrimp, 6, 32–33
skull bones and hearing, 12, 13, 31
snakes, 12, 18
snowshoe hare, **12**
sonar, 24, 47
sonic boom, 9, 47
sound recording: and acoustic monitoring, 18–19, 36, 39–41; archiving, 23; digital, **6**, 18–19, 38–39, **40**, **42**; hydrophones, **22**; phonautograph, 14, 38, 47; spectrographs, **19**
soundscape, 16–17, 47
soundscape ecology: acoustic monitoring, 18–19, 36, 39–41; and conservation, 35, 40, 43–44; defined, 47; listening to nature, 20, 37, 44
sound waves: frequency, 8, 9, 31, 46; history of, 8–9; in a vacuum, 9, 47
spectrogram, 39, 47

sperm whale, 13
spiders, 10
squirrels, 20–21
stridulate, 6, 20, 47

Tanzania, national park, **22**
tarsiers, 9, 32
telephone, 14–15
thrushes, **30**
tiger moth, 36
tigers, **32**
tiger shark, **13**
tobacco plants, 12
tomato plants, 12

ultrasonic sound waves, 12, **24**, 47
ultrasound, 31, 32, 47
urban noise, **17**, 27–28, 29, 30

vacuum, 9, 47
vocalizations: animal behaviors, 7, 14; aquatic, 13, 24; bioacoustics, 17–18, 46; frequencies of, 9, 31; mechanisms, 10

whales, 13, 14, 24, **25**, 31, 37
white-tailed deer, 7
Wild Sanctuary, 23, 42
World Soundscape Project (WSP), 22–23
wrens, 44

yellow parasitic fly, 33

zebra finch, 30
Zion National Park (Utah), 43

49

Acknowledgments

A chorus of people helped make this book possible. A shout-out to Kirstie Hudson and the rest of the ensemble of editors at Orca Book Publishers for singing along page by page, and to the rest of the orchestra at Orca for transforming it from words on a page to performance art. Special thanks to my agent, Stacey Kondla, for keeping me in tune as this book unfolded.

It has been delightful to work with the flock of fantastic photographers who contributed their talent and expertise to this book, especially Rhonda Himes, Len Modderman and John Davidson, who searched their files to find just the right photos to match the melody. To my friend and colleague Dr. Ole Hendrickson, thank you for scouring the manuscript, cross-checking the science and providing your suggestions. To sweet Reta for being the sounding board for repeated readings and for listening to all the stories I excitedly shared.

Finally, to all the living voices in our natural world who make our planet musical and delightfully habitable: May every human being learn to listen to you and learn how to tread softly on this precious earth.

ELLEN REITMAN

STEPHEN AITKEN is a biologist, artist and science writer. After completing an honors biology degree with a minor in fine arts and spending some time at the Carleton School of Architecture, Stephen went on to have a career as a biological illustrator, editor and writer. He has been creating his own children's books for the past 15 years. Stephen's books and articles are inspired by the wonders of the natural world. He is the co-founder and executive secretary of the charity Biodiversity Conservancy International and senior editor of the journal Biodiversity.

ORCA FOOTPRINTS

The more you know, the more you grow.

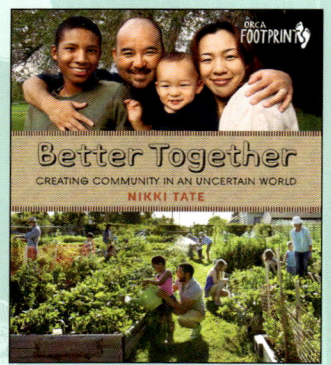
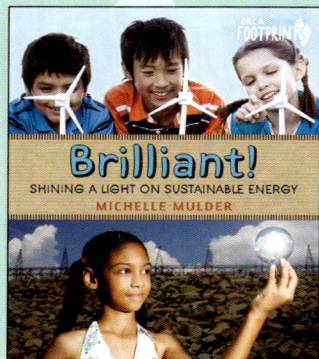
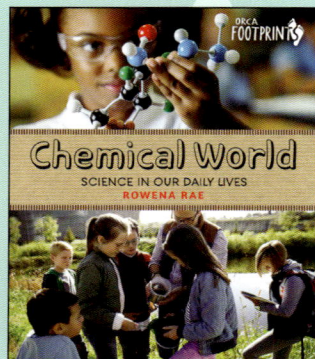
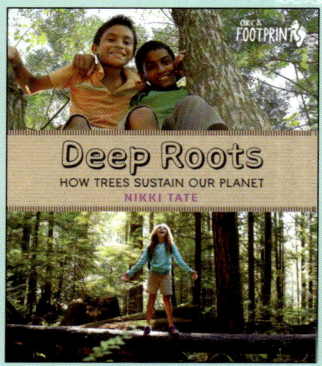
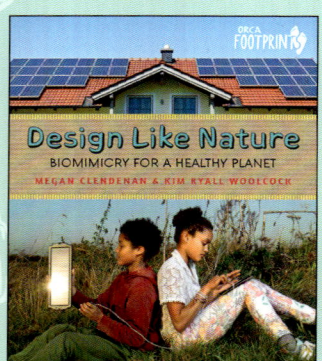
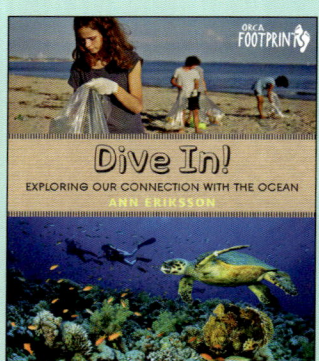

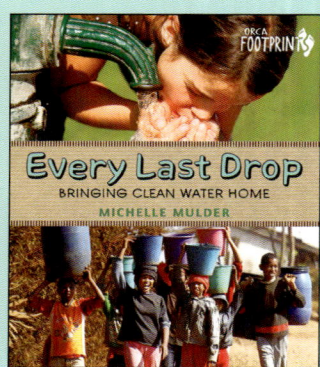
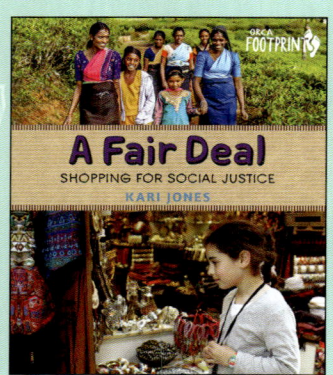
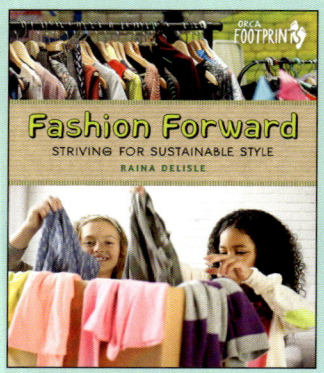
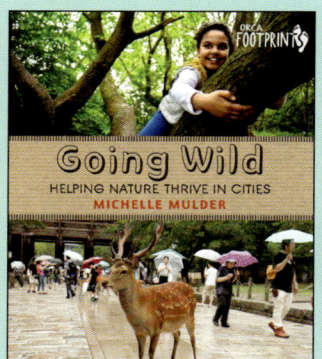

★ "Fascinating."
—*School Library Journal*, starred review for *Design Like Nature*